YOGA FOR EVERYONE

SEATED YOGA

BY LAURA VILLANO, RYT
ILLUSTRATED BY CHRISTOS SKALTSAS

TIPS FOR CAREGIVERS

The practice of yoga helps us learn about our breath and body, how the two are connected, and how they can help us acknowledge our feelings without letting them overwhelm us. This awareness can help us navigate different situations at school or at home. Yoga gives us tools to be the best versions of ourselves in every situation. Plus, moving our bodies feels good!

SOCIAL AND EMOTIONAL GOALS

After reading this book, kids will be able to use their yoga practice to:

1. Become more aware of their emotions and the physical sensations they produce in the body (self-awareness).
2. Use the techniques included in the text to help manage their emotions and de-stress (self-management).

TIPS FOR PRACTICE

Encourage self-awareness and self-management with these prompts:

Before reading: Ask students to check in with themselves. How do they feel, in both mind and body?
Emotional example: What kinds of thoughts are you having?
Physical example: How does your body feel today?

During reading: Encourage students to check in as they move through the book.
Emotional example: How does it feel when you close your eyes and focus on your breathing?
Physical example: How do certain poses feel in your body?

After reading: Take time to reflect after practicing the poses.
Emotional example: How do you feel after practicing yoga?
Physical example: Are there certain poses you like or don't like?

TABLE OF CONTENTS

BEFORE YOU BEGIN YOUR PRACTICE, YOU WILL NEED:

- Yoga mat (A towel or blanket works, too!)
- Comfy clothes so you can move around easily
- Water to stay hydrated
- A good attitude and an open mind!

By practicing the poses in this book, you understand any physical activity has some risk of injury. If you experience pain or discomfort, please listen to your body, discontinue activity, and ask for help.

CHAPTER 1

WHAT IS YOGA?

Namaste (nah-mah-stay)! This is how we greet each other when we practice **yoga**. When people say it, they often place their palms together in front of their chest and slightly bow their head.

Yoga is a **sequence** of body movements. It can help us sleep better and **focus**. It also builds muscle and helps us be more **flexible**. Let's practice seated yoga!

CHAPTER 2

LET'S PRACTICE!

- Start seated on your mat.
- Cross your legs.
- Focus on keeping your back straight.
- Draw your shoulders down your back.
- Rest your arms by your sides or in your lap.

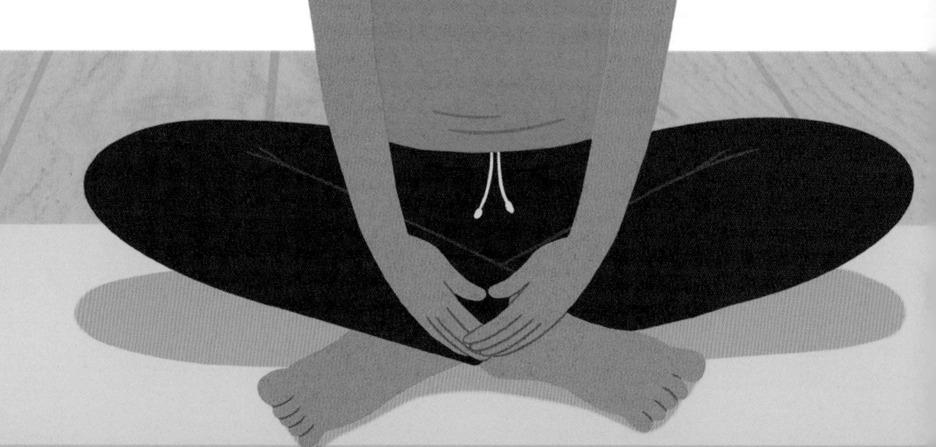

It is important to pay attention to your breathing as you practice yoga.

- Put your hand on your stomach.
- **Inhale** through your nose. Feel the air enter your nose and fill up your belly.
- Then **exhale**. Feel your belly relax as the air leaves your nose.
- Repeat this 10 times.

Practice moving your body with your breath.

- Reach your arms overhead as you inhale.
- Exhale and lower your arms back to your sides.
- Repeat this 5 times.

DID YOU KNOW?

Yoga was developed more than 5,000 years ago in India. Now, people all around the world practice it.

BUTTERFLY POSE

- Sit with the bottoms of your feet touching.
- Drop your knees toward your mat or the floor. Your legs will make a diamond shape.
- Wrap your hands around your feet.
- Start with your back straight.
- Inhale.
- As you exhale, lean forward.

TIP: Try bringing your feet closer to you. How does this change the stretch? Find the right position for your body!

FORWARD FOLD

- Sit tall. Extend your legs. **Flex** your toes.
- Inhale and reach your arms over your head.
- As you exhale, start to fold forward. Reach your fingers toward your toes.
- Fold forward with a straight back. When you feel your back start to round, you've folded far enough!
- Hold this **pose** for 5 breaths.

HEAD-TO-KNEE FORWARD BEND

- Inhale and rise back up to a seated position.
- Rest your left foot on the inside of your right thigh.
- Inhale as you reach your arms up and overhead.
- Exhale and fold forward over your right knee.
- Reach your hands to your right foot. Bring your head toward your right knee.
- Now try the other side! Do you notice anything different between the two sides?

TIP: Try bending your right knee. How does this change the stretch? Can you touch your forehead to your knee?

BOAT POSE

- Bring your feet out in front of you.
- Bend your knees.
- Keep your back straight. Focus on your belly muscles.
- Grab the backs of your thighs.
- Slowly lift both feet off of the floor or mat. This is Boat Pose!

TIP: Try to straighten one leg at a time. How does this feel?

SEATED TWIST

- Sit tall and extend your legs in front of you. Let's try a twist!
- Keep your right leg straight.
- Bend your left knee and cross it over your right leg. Rest your left foot flat on the floor or mat.
- Wrap your right arm around your left knee and twist to the left.
- Rest your left hand on the floor behind you. How does this pose feel?
- Release the twist and try it on the other side!

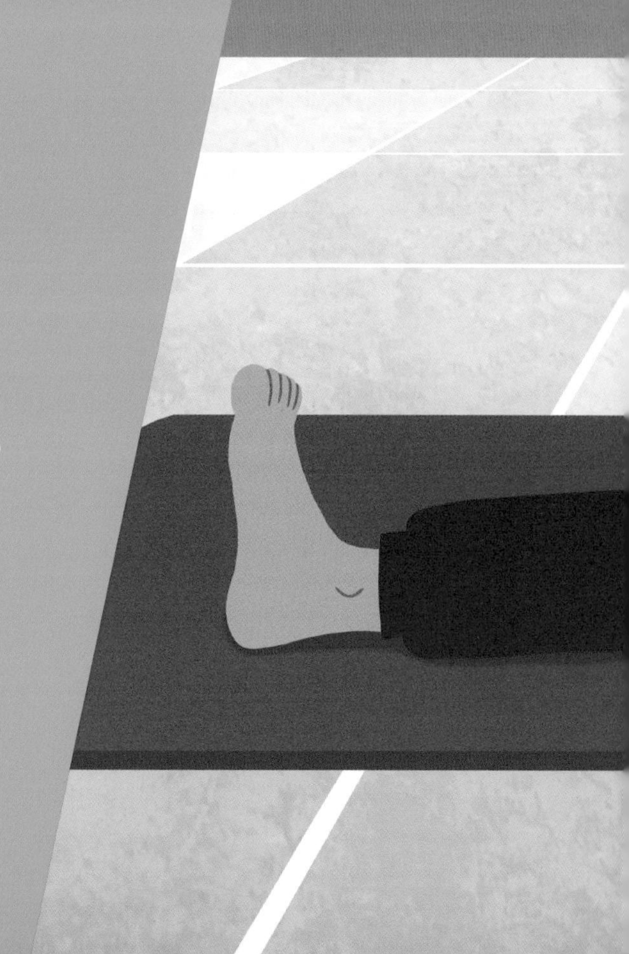

CHAPTER 3

REFLECT

Let's finish our seated yoga practice!

- Lie down on your back.
- If it feels comfortable, close your eyes.
- Inhale and exhale 5 times.

How do you feel? Take some time to **reflect** on your seated yoga practice.

Namaste!

GOALS AND TOOLS

GROW WITH GOALS

Practice bringing yoga into your everyday life. This can look different for everyone. Here are some ideas to get you started. You can set your own goals, too!

1. Folding forward can look and feel different for everyone. When you practice a pose regularly, it can start to look and feel different in your body. Try this with your Forward Fold. Practice every day for a week. See what happens when you do this stretch every day! What changes?
2. Boat Pose works the muscles in your stomach. Practice Boat Pose every day for a week. Hold it for 10 seconds each time. Then try increasing the amount of time you hold it the next week. Keep adding on!

TRY THIS!

Play Yogi, Yogi, Go! (Just like Duck, Duck, Goose!)

1. Sit in a circle with a group of friends or classmates.
2. Have everyone sit in Butterfly Pose.
3. One friend starts and moves around the circle tapping friends on the head, saying, "Yogi, Yogi" and picks someone by saying, "Go!"
4. The first child will run around the circle trying to make it back to his or her seat without getting tagged.
5. If tagged, that child has to hold Boat Pose in the middle of the circle until everyone counts to 10. You can try a different pose each time!

GLOSSARY

exhale
To breathe out.

flex
To move or tense a muscle by contraction.

flexible
Able to bend.

focus
To concentrate on something.

inhale
To breathe in.

namaste
A common greeting in yoga. It means, "The spirit in me honors and acknowledges the spirit in you."

pose
A position or posture.

reflect
To think carefully or seriously about something.

sequence
A series or collection of things that follow each other in a particular order.

yoga
A system of exercises and meditation that helps people control their minds and bodies and become physically fit.

TO LEARN MORE

Finding more information is as easy as 1, 2, 3.

1. Go to www.factsurfer.com
2. Enter "**seatedyoga**" into the search box.
3. Choose your cover to see a list of websites.

INDEX

Blue Owl Books are published by Jump!, 5357 Penn Avenue South, Minneapolis, MN 55419, www.jumplibrary.com

Library of Congress Cataloging-in-Publication Data is available at www.loc.gov or upon request from the publisher.

ISBN: 978-1-64527-187-1 (hardcover)
ISBN: 978-1-64527-188-8 (paperback)
ISBN: 978-1-64527-189-5 (ebook)

Editor: Jenna Trnka
Designer: Anna Peterson
Illustrator: Christos Skaltsas

Printed in the United States of America at Corporate Graphics in North Mankato, Minnesota.